Camille

A Travesty on
La Dame aux Camélias
by Alexandre Dumas Fils

by Charles Ludlam

A SAMUEL FRENCH ACTING EDITION

NEW YORK HOLLYWOOD LONDON TORONTO

SAMUELFRENCH.COM

Copyright © 1989 by the Estate of Charles Ludlam
ALL RIGHTS RESERVED

CAUTION: Professionals and amateurs are hereby warned that *CAMILLE* is subject to a Licensing Fee. It is fully protected under the copyright laws of the United States of America, the British Commonwealth, including Canada, and all other countries of the Copyright Union. All rights, including professional, amateur, motion picture, recitation, lecturing, public reading, radio broadcasting, television and the rights of translation into foreign languages are strictly reserved. In its present form the play is dedicated to the reading public only.

The amateur and professional live stage performance rights to *CAMILLE* are controlled exclusively by Samuel French, Inc., and licensing arrangements and performance licenses must be secured well in advance of presentation. PLEASE NOTE that amateur Licensing Fees are set upon application in accordance with your producing circumstances. When applying for a licensing quotation and a performance license please give us the number of performances intended, dates of production, your seating capacity and admission fee. Licensing Fees are payable one week before the opening performance of the play to Samuel French, Inc., at 45 W. 25th Street, New York, NY 10010.

Licensing Fee of the required amount must be paid whether the play is presented for charity or gain and whether or not admission is charged.

Stock licensing fees quoted upon application to Samuel French, Inc.

For all other rights than those stipulated above, apply to: Fitelson, Lasky, Aslan & Couture, 551 Fifth Avenue, New York, NY 10176, (212) 586-4700, attn: Jerold Couture.

Particular emphasis is laid on the question of amateur or professional readings, permission and terms for which must be secured in writing from Samuel French, Inc.

Copying from this book in whole or in part is strictly forbidden by law, and the right of performance is not transferable.

Whenever the play is produced the following notice must appear on all programs, printing and advertising for the play: "Produced by special arrangement with Samuel French, Inc."

Due authorship credit must be given on all programs, printing and advertising for the play.

ISBN 978-0-573-69863-7   Printed in U.S.A.   #5243

No one shall commit or authorize any act or omission by which the copyright of, or the right to copyright, this play may be impaired.

No one shall make any changes in this play for the purpose of production.

Publication of this play does not imply availability for performance. Both amateurs and professionals considering a production are strongly advised in their own interests to apply to Samuel French, Inc., for written permission before starting rehearsals, advertising, or booking a theatre.

No part of this book may be reproduced, stored in a retrieval system, or transmitted in any form, by any means, now known or yet to be invented, including mechanical, electronic, photocopying, recording, videotaping, or otherwise, without the prior written permission of the publisher.

MUSIC USE NOTE

Licensees are solely responsible for obtaining formal written permission from copyright owners to use copyrighted music in the performance of this play and are strongly cautioned to do so. If no such permission is obtained by the licensee, then the licensee must use only original music that the licensee owns and controls. Licensees are solely responsible and liable for all music clearances and shall indemnify the copyright owners of the play and their licensing agent, Samuel French, Inc., against any costs, expenses, losses and liabilities arising from the use of music by licensees.

IMPORTANT BILLING AND CREDIT REQUIREMENTS

All producers of *CAMILLE must* give credit to the Author of the Play in all programs distributed in connection with performances of the Play, and in all instances in which the title of the Play appears for the purposes of advertising, publicizing or otherwise exploiting the Play and/or a production. The name of the Author *must* appear on a separate line on which no other name appears, immediately following the title and *must* appear in size of type not less than fifty percent of the size of the title type.

CAMILLE was produced by the Ridiculous Theatrical Company at the Evergreen Theatre on May 13, 1974. The performance was directed by Charles Ludlam, with sets by Bobjack Callejo, costumes by Mary Brecht, and lighting by Richard Currie. The production stage managers were Richard Gibbs and Doug Schwegler. The cast was as follows:

BARON DE VARVILLE	John D. Brockmeyer
NANINE	Jack Mallory
MARGUERITE GAUTIER	Charles Ludlam
BUTLER	Stephen Sterne
NICHETTE FONDUE	George Osterman
OLYMPE DE TAVERNE	Black-Eyed Susan
SAINT GAUDENS	Robert Reddy
PRUDENCE DUVERNOY	Lola Pashalinski
GASTON ROUÉ	Robert Beers
ARMAND DUVAL	Bill Vehr
DUVAL SENIOR	Richard Currie

CHARACTERS

BARON DE VARVILLE, Armand's rival
NANINE, maid
MARGUERITE GAUTIER, a courtesan
JOSEPH, the butler
NICHETTE FONDUE, a childhood friend of Marguerite
OLYMPE DE TAVERNE, Saint Gaudens's mistress
SAINT GAUDENS, a roué
PRUDENCE DUVERNOY, a milliner
GASTON ROUÉ, a playboy
ARMAND DUVAL, Marguerite's lover
DUVAL SR, Armand's father

SETTING

Marguerite's drawing room. Paris.

TIME

1848

ACT I

(**MARGUERITE**'s *drawing room. Paris, 1848.*)

VARVILLE. *(pacing up and down with a bouquet of flowers)* Will she see me?

NANINE. Madame says she wants to be alone.

VARVILLE. So, she's playing cat and mouse, eh? Well, I hope she finds him amusing, whoever he is.

NANINE. Madame is alone. She has seen no one for three days. She's been ill again. It's a pathetic story....

VARVILLE. Oh, yes, that is a pathetic story. Only unfortunately...

NANINE. Unfortunately?

VARVILLE. Unfortunately, I don't believe it.

NANINE. There are enough true things that can be said about Madame, so there's no use your telling things that aren't true. Madame never tells lies.

VARVILLE. *(laughs)* Of course not.

NANINE. During her long illness, Madame accumulated over fifty thousand francs' worth of debts, and that's no lie.

VARVILLE. Bring Madame these flowers and tell her I am offering to pay her debts. Is it my fault I love her?

NANINE. *(taking the flowers)* I don't know. It may be better to owe money to some people than gratitude to others.

(**NANINE** *exits into* **MARGUERITE**'s *room with the flowers. Off:*)

Marguerite, the Baron de Varville is still waiting. He says he is willing to pay all your debts if you will only see him. And he sends these flowers.

VARVILLE. Birds of paradise and aspidistra.

MARGUERITE. Aagh, get them away from me! Get those flowers away from me!

(The bouquet of flowers comes flying out of the door.)

VARVILLE. *(picking them up)* You don't care for them?

MARGUERITE. What do they call me?

VARVILLE. Why...er...ah...you are called many things that one would hesitate to repeat.

MARGUERITE. I mean my name. What is my name?

VARVILLE. Marguerite Gautier.

MARGUERITE. No, no, you fool. I mean by what name am I known in the Bohemian quarter?

VARVILLE. The Lady of the Camellias.

MARGUERITE. *(enters)* Why?

VARVILLE. Because you wear no other flowers?

MARGUERITE. And I can bear no other flowers. Their scent makes me ill. *(coughs)* Now take your birds of paradise and get your ass-padistra out of here.

(VARVILLE does not move.)

You're not going?

VARVILLE. No.

MARGUERITE. Then, for God's sake, play the piano, dahling. Your music is your only saving grace.

VARVILLE. *(obeying)* Is it my fault I love you?

MARGUERITE. If I were to listen to everyone who's in love with me, I would have no time for dinner. *(to NANINE)* Did you order dinner?

NANINE. Yes, Madame.

MARGUERITE. *(to VARVILLE)* I let you call on me when I'm in and wait for me when I'm out. But if you insist on talking of nothing but your love, I will withdraw my friendship.

VARVILLE. What have you got against love?

MARGUERITE. I have nothing against love. It just makes such dull conversation.

VARVILLE. And yet, last year at Marienbad you did give me some hope.

MARGUERITE. My dear, that was last year, that was Marienbad. I was ill; I was bored. But this is Paris and I'm very much better, and not at all bored.

NANINE. Marguerite, the doctor called again this morning.

MARGUERITE. What did he say?

NANINE. He said you are to rest as much as possible.

MARGUERITE. Dear doctor, always giving me good advice. *(to* **VARVILLE***)* What's that you're playing?

VARVILLE. A rhapsody by Rauschenberg.

MARGUERITE. It's charming.

VARVILLE. Listen, Marguerite, I have eighty thousand francs.

MARGUERITE. How nice. I have a hundred thousand.

VARVILLE. Your indifference to me is like a camellia, no scent and no thorns.

MARGUERITE. *(aside to* **NANINE***)* He is the most persistent man in Paris. He insists on loving me.

NANINE. *(confidentially)* He has eighty thousand francs.

MARGUERITE. How he bores me with his eighty thousand francs.

(The bell rings. **BUTLER** *goes to the door.)*

BUTLER. *(announcing)* Nichette Fondue.

NICHETTE. Marguerite!

MARGUERITE. Nichette!

NICHETTE. You're looking well.

MARGUERITE. I always look well when I'm near death. Will you stay for supper?

NICHETTE. I can't. Gustave is waiting downstairs.

MARGUERITE. Oh, Nichette, you're still seeing that Gustave?

NICHETTE. Yes. He's been promoted to com*p*-troller!

MARGUERITE. Oh, Nichette, you can do much better than a comptroller!

NICHETTE. But I never want to do better than Gustave. I love him.

MARGUERITE. Nichette, you're a very pretty girl, but a very bad businesswoman.

NICHETTE. You'll see, Marguerite. One of these days you'll fall like a ton of bricks.

MARGUERITE. Me, fall in love? No, no, Nichette!

NICHETTE. Toodle-oo, Marguerite.

MARGUERITE. Ta-ta, Nichette.

(bell)

BUTLER. *(announcing)* Madame Olympe de Taverné. Monsieur Saint Gaudens.

MARGUERITE. At last, Olympe. I thought you weren't coming.

OLYMPE. Blame it on Saint Gaudens. It's his fault.

SAINT GAUDENS. It's always my fault. Good evening, Marguerite. Good evening, Varville.

OLYMPE. I just found out today that Saint Gaudens is of Polish extraction.

MARGUERITE. No.

OLYMPE. His dentist is Polish. *(aside to* **MARGUERITE***)* Did you invite Gaylord?

MARGUERITE. I thought you would bring him.

OLYMPE. With Saint Gaudens? You know how jealous he is.

MARGUERITE. I thought you had him trained.

OLYMPE. You can't teach an old dog new tricks.

MARGUERITE. I like older men. They're so...grateful.

OLYMPE. And they have so much...poise.

SAINT GAUDENS. Is Varville staying for supper?

MARGUERITE. No, he isn't. He's being punished for bringing me the wrong flowers.

SAINT GAUDENS. Didn't he bring camellias?

MARGUERITE. No, he didn't.

OLYMPE. How gouache of him. He committed a real false pah!

SAINT GAUDENS. Varville's in the doghouse.

MARGUERITE. *(yelling out the window)* Prudence!

PRUDENCE. *(off)* What do you want?

MARGUERITE. I want you to come over here at once.

PRUDENCE. Why?

MARGUERITE. Because it's my birthday and the Baron de Varville is still here, and he's boring me to death.

PRUDENCE. I have two young gentlemen here who have asked me out to supper.

MARGUERITE. Well, bring them over here to supper. Anything is better than the Baron. Who are they?

PRUDENCE. You know one of them, Gaston Roué.

MARGUERITE. Of course I know him. And the other?

PRUDENCE. A friend of his.

MARGUERITE. Come on over, dahlings, there's plenty of food here.

OLYMPE. It's so convenient to have Prudence living just across the courtyard.

MARGUERITE. Yes, she delivers my gossip fresh every morning.

SAINT GAUDENS. Who is this Prudence?

OLYMPE. She was once a kept woman who tried to go on the stage and failed. So, relying on her acquaintance with fashionable people, she opened a milliner's shop.

MARGUERITE. And nobody buys her hats but me.

OLYMPE. But you never wear them.

MARGUERITE. Dahling, they're beastly. I wouldn't wear one to a dogfight. But I adore Prudence, and she is hard up. *(coughs a little)* It's cold this evening.

(A bell rings.)

BUTLER. *(at the door)* Madame Prudence Duvernoy, Monsieur Gaston Roué, and Monsieur Armand Duval.

PRUDENCE. *(barges in wearing a big hat)* The classy way they announce people here! I knew this party was going to be piss elegant!

GASTON. *(to* **MARGUERITE**, *kissing her hand)* I trust you are well, Madame.

MARGUERITE. Quite well, thank you. And you?

PRUDENCE. Gee, the classy way they talk here! Marguerite, I want to present to you Monsieur Armand Duval, the man who is more in love with you than any man in Paris.

MARGUERITE. Nanine, set two more places. I hope his great passion hasn't spoiled Monsieur Duval's appetite.

ARMAND. Please accept this book as a remembrance of your birthday.

MARGUERITE. *Manon Lescaut?*

ARMAND. Yes. The story of a woman who brightened her wit with champagne, and her eyes with tears.

MARGUERITE. It's not a sad story, is it? I don't like sad thoughts.

ARMAND. It has a sad ending.

MARGUERITE. Well, I'll read it, but I won't read the ending.

SAINT GAUDENS. My dear Gaston, I'm so glad to see you!

GASTON. Saint Gaudens…as young as ever!

SAINT GAUDENS. Younger. Only my teeth are aging.

GASTON. And your love affairs – prospering?

SAINT GAUDENS. Well, there's Olympe here.

GASTON. So, you've taken up with this little trollop, eh?

OLYMPE. Watch who you call little.

MARGUERITE. *(to* **NANINE**, *who is setting the table)* Not the Melmac, Nanine, the Limoges.

GASTON. Whatever became of Beatrice?

SAINT GAUDENS. I gave her up. Her lover was a banker but she loved me for myself alone. But, still, the affair required a lot of hiding in cupboards, prowling about the back stairs, and waiting in the street.

GASTON. Which gave you rheumatism.

SAINT GAUDENS. Not a bit, but times change. We none of us grows any younger.

GASTON. *(to* **MARGUERITE***)* Isn't he wonderful?

MARGUERITE. We are all growing old at exactly the same rate so there will be no sympathy for anyone, do you hear? *(to* **ARMAND***)* Are you following me?

ARMAND. Yes.

SAINT GAUDENS. *(to* **ARMAND***)* Are you related to Monsieur Duval, the receiver general?

ARMAND. Yes, sir, he is my father. Do you know him?

SAINT GAUDENS. I met him years ago at the Marchioness Fanzeepanzee's summer house, with your mother whom I remember as a very beautiful and charming fairy of a woman. You take after your mother.

ARMAND. My mother died three years ago.

SAINT GAUDENS. Forgive me.

ARMAND. I am always glad to be reminded of my mother.

SAINT GAUDENS. Are you an only son?

ARMAND. I have one sister....

*(***ARMAND***,* **SAINT GAUDENS***, and* **OLYMPE** *join* **VARVILLE** *at the piano.)*

MARGUERITE. *(aside to* **GASTON***)* I think your friend is charming.

GASTON. He is and, what's more, he adores you. Doesn't he, Prudence?

PRUDENCE. What?

GASTON. I was telling Marguerite that Armand is madly in love with her.

PRUDENCE. He's got it bad and that ain't good. Ah, l'amour, l'amour!

GASTON. He loves you so much, my dear, that he doesn't dare tell you about it.

MARGUERITE. Varville, please!

VARVILLE. *(banging the piano keys)* You told me to play the piano.

MARGUERITE. When I am alone with you, not when I have friends.

PRUDENCE. He's loved you for two years.

MARGUERITE. Quite an old story, then.

GASTON. Armand simply lives at Gustave's and Nichette's to hear them talk about you.

PRUDENCE. I want something to drink.

OLYMPE. Look, I found some champagne.

(PRUDENCE, GASTON, and OLYMPE get involved in opening the bottle of champagne.)

NANINE. *(taking MARGUERITE aside)* Marguerite, when you were ill a year ago, remember I told you of a young man who called to inquire after you every day but wouldn't leave his name?

MARGUERITE. I remember.

NANINE. *(pointing discreetly)* That's him. Armand Duval.

MARGUERITE. How nice of him. *(calling across the room)* Monsieur Duval, do you know what I have just been hearing? That you called to inquire after me every day when I was ill.

ARMAND. It's quite true.

MARGUERITE. Then the least I can do is thank you. Did you hear that, Varville? *You* never did that for me, did you?

VARVILLE. I have only known you for a year.

MARGUERITE. Don't be ridiculous, this young gentleman has only known me for five minutes.

BUTLER. *(enters with boar's head on platter)* Dinner is served. *(exits)*

PRUDENCE. Here is supper. I'm famished.

VARVILLE. I have no luck. Good-bye, Marguerite Gautier, Lady of the Camellias. *(kisses her hand)*

MARGUERITE. Good-bye. When shall we see you again?

VARVILLE. Whenever you wish. *(bowing)* Gentlemen. *(exits)*

SAINT GAUDENS. Good-bye, Varville, old boy. Better luck next time.

MARGUERITE. Let's eat!

(They rush madly to the table.)

PRUDENCE. You really are too hard on the Baron, dear. You could end up a baroness if you played your cards right. We're none of us getting any younger, and it's time you settled something about your future – while you still have one!

OLYMPE. I simply adore the Baron. He's rich, handsome, wealthy, talented, and he's got money! Do you know that he's just written a book?

MARGUERITE. Really?

GASTON. Ah, yes, his memoirs are considered the breviary of The Decadence.

PRUDENCE. And he's got eighty thousand francs.

MARGUERITE. How he bores me with his eighty thousand francs.

OLYMPE. Eighty thousand francs! I wish someone would offer to bore me that way! Do you know what Saint Gaudens gave me for my birthday? A coupé! But he didn't give me any horses to go with it!

PRUDENCE. Still, a coupé is a coupé is a coupé!

ALL. *(clinking glasses simultaneously)* Touché!

SAINT GAUDENS. I'm ruined. Why can't I be loved for myself alone?

OLYMPE. *(shrieking with laughter)* The idea!

MARGUERITE. Oh, come on Saint Gaudens, come and get your MDA.

SAINT GAUDENS. What's MDA?

MARGUERITE. Monsieur, don't ask.

PRUDENCE. What are those little fellows?

GASTON. Partridges.

PRUDENCE. *(to BUTLER)* You can put some on my plate.

GASTON. Some? Partridges aren't oysters, you know.

PRUDENCE. Well, they're not much bigger than oysters.

GASTON. What a birdlike appetite. Now we know who ruined Saint Gaudens…she did!

PRUDENCE. She! She! Is that any way to talk of a lady? Why in my day…

GASTON. We needn't go back to Louis the Fifteenth! Marguerite, fill Armand's glass. He's looking sad.

SAINT GAUDENS. This dinner is delicious.

PRUDENCE. I want another drink.

MARGUERITE. Gaston, play the piano. Come on, Saint Gaudens, sing us a song.

SAINT GAUDENS. How can I sing when I'm having my supper?

MARGUERITE. Sing for your supper.

PRUDENCE. I want another drink!

(**SAINT GAUDENS** *begins to sing "Plaisir d'Amour."*)

MARGUERITE. No, no, not that one! Let's have something gay, dahling.

(**SAINT GAUDENS** *sings "Frère Jacques" and all join him, singing in rounds.*)

ALL. Bravo! Bravo! *(taps glasses with silverware)* Toast!

GASTON. *(making a toast)* Ah, life is short and sweet and Prudence is short and fat.

(All clink their glasses together and drink.)

PRUDENCE. *(quite drunk)* I want another drink!

OLYMPE. Fat, fair, and forty!

PRUDENCE. All right, smart ass, how old do you think I am? I'm…thirty-six!

(riotous laughter)

GASTON. But you don't look a day over forty!

PRUDENCE. I've been told I have the skin of a thirteen-year old.

OLYMPE. Well, you better give it back, you're getting it wrinkled.

(**PRUDENCE** *grimaces and then more riotous laughter.*)

(**PRUDENCE** *hits* **GASTON** *over the head with a partridge.* **SAINT GAUDENS** *whispers in* **OLYMPE**'s *ear.*)

OLYMPE. *(shrieking with laughter)* That's the funniest story I've ever heard in my life!

PRUDENCE. Tell me! Tell me! *(motioning to* **SAINT GAUDENS***)* Whisper in my ear.

MARGUERITE. That isn't fair. Tell us all. We want to hear it too.

PRUDENCE. *(laughing almost uncontrollably)* I know what's coming, but do go on.

MARGUERITE. I want to hear it too.

SAINT GAUDENS. You tell her, Gaston.

GASTON. Ah, but you tell it so much better than I do.

SAINT GAUDENS. But it's your story.

GASTON. But I like to hear you tell it.

MARGUERITE. *(shouts in a masculine voice)* Let's have the story, man. Out with it!

OLYMPE. If Saint Gaudens won't tell it, I will.

SAINT GAUDENS. *(cupping his hand over her mouth)* I'll tell it! I'll tell it! Well, you remember that awful divorce last year of Odile de Lille and that stockbroker of hers. Well, last week I saw her at the Ballet Gala at the Opera. They were doing *Zinnia, The Mute Girl of Cincinnati.* And who should arrive in the next box but Odile's ex! And he leaned over and said in a very loud voice, "Odile, my dear, how does your new husband like that worn-out twat of yours?" And she said –

OLYMPE. *(breaking loose and interrupting)* "He likes it fine, once he gets past the worn-out part!"

(Everyone laughs uproariously except **ARMAND.***)*

MARGUERITE. Monsieur Duval, you're not laughing. Don't you like Gaston's jokes?

ARMAND. I have heard Gaston's jokes. In fact, he learned some of them from me. But I would rather they were not repeated in your presence.

*(***OLYPME** *does a spit take.)*

MARGUERITE. Come now, I'm not a colonel's daughter just out of the convent.

SAINT GAUDENS. Who hasn't been deceived? One's friends and one's mistresses are always deceiving one.

PRUDENCE. Ah yes, just as in *Berenice* by Racine…

*(**PRUDENCE** takes center stage, gesturing madly and emitting Gallic gutturals. The others look at her in wonderment.)*

MARGUERITE. Oh, she's acting.

PRUDENCE. Oh, mon pauvre chevrolet. J'aime le chateaubriand. Oh, le coq au vin, le coq au vin, sur le table avec les pommes frites.

*(Standing at the table, she leans back on top of it, in a kind of reverie. **GASTON** throws a pie in her face. Everyone laughs.)*

MARGUERITE. Bravo, Saint Gaudens. You are a hero and we are all in love with you. All those madly in love with Saint Gaudens hold up your hands. *(to **SAINT GAUDENS**)* Well, hold up your hand, dahling. Unanimous. Prudence, my dear, you really ought to stick to Maeterlinck. You will always be remembered for your *Joiselle*. Gaston, play something for Saint Gaudens to dance to.

GASTON. I don't know anything but St. Vitus' Dance.

MARGUERITE. Then we'll have St. Vitus' Dance. Come on, Saint Gaudens…Armand, move the table.

PRUDENCE. But I haven't finished.

OLYMPE. Do I have to dance with Saint Gaudens?

MARGUERITE. No, I'm going to. Come along, little Saint Gaudens.

ARMAND. Aren't you afraid that you're not well enough to dance?

MARGUERITE. I'm not afraid of anything except being bored.

OLYMPE. Come, Armand.

SAINT GAUDENS. Your hollandaise was divine, my dear.

MARGUERITE. It's especially good around the Jewish hollandaise.

(All dance to the music that **GASTON** *plays.* **MARGUERITE** *coughs. The music stops. All look to her.)*

SAINT GAUDENS. What's the matter?

MARGUERITE. Nothing. I lost my breath.

ARMAND. *(going to her)* Are you all right?

MARGUERITE. Yes. It's nothing. Don't stop. *(Starts to dance again and then falls.)*

ARMAND. Stop, Gaston.

PRUDENCE. Marguerite is ill.

MARGUERITE. It's nothing. *(falls again)*

ARMAND. *(catching her)* The party's over.

PRUDENCE. She's always ill just when everybody is having a good time.

OLYMPE. You can never have any fun here.

PRUDENCE. Let's go somewhere else. Let's go to my place. Wait a minute! I'm just beginning to get hungry again! Bring the food with us. Forward…march!

GASTON. *(to* **ARMAND***)* She's been laughing too much and she's spitting up blood. It's nothing. It happens to her every day.

(Exit all with the food except **MARGUERITE** *and* **ARMAND***.)*

MARGUERITE. *(looking a mirror)* How pale I look!

ARMAND. You're killing yourself.

MARGUERITE. If I am, you're the only one who objects. The others don't worry about me.

ARMAND. The others don't love you as I do.

MARGUERITE. Ah yes, I had forgotten that great love of yours.

ARMAND. You laugh at it.

MARGUERITE. I've heard it too many times to laugh anymore. It's an old joke and the joke is on me.

ARMAND. Promise.

MARGUERITE. What?

ARMAND. To take care of yourself.

MARGUERITE. My good man, if I were to begin to take care of myself, I would die. Don't you see that it is only the feverish life I live that keeps me alive? The moment that I am no longer amusing to people, they leave me, and the long days are followed by longer nights. I know, I was in bed for two months and after three weeks, no one came near me.

ARMAND. Those people are horrible.

MARGUERITE. They're the only friends I have and I'm no better than they are.

ARMAND. Don't say that. Let me take you away from all this. We could go to the country where I would take care of you like a brother. I'd never leave you and I would cure you. Then, when you were strong again, you could return to this life if you wished, but I don't think you would want to.

MARGUERITE. How depressing. I don't like sad thoughts.

ARMAND. Have you no heart, Marguerite?

MARGUERITE. I'm traveling light, no heart.

ARMAND. Have you never been in love with anyone?

MARGUERITE. *(exaggerating the word)* Nevvv…aaiirr!!!!!!

ARMAND. Thank God!

MARGUERITE. You're a strange boy. You've drunk too much wine and that has made you sentimental. Tomorrow it will be a different story.

ARMAND. Was it wine that brought me here every day when you were ill?

MARGUERITE. No, that couldn't have been wine. But why didn't you come up?

ARMAND. What right had I?

MARGUERITE. Since when are men so formal with women like me!

ARMAND. And I was afraid.

MARGUERITE. Afraid?

ARMAND. Afraid that you would grant me too promptly that which I wanted to win through long suffering and great sacrifice. Imagination lends too much poetry to the senses, and the desires of the body make concessions to the dreams of the soul. I would rather die for your love than pay fifty francs for it.

MARGUERITE. So, it's as bad as that! And you would look after me?

ARMAND. Yes.

MARGUERITE. You would stay with me all day long?

ARMAND. Yes.

MARGUERITE. And even all night?

ARMAND. As long as I didn't weary you.

MARGUERITE. And what does this great devotion come from!

ARMAND. The irresistible sympathy which I have for you.

MARGUERITE. So you are in love with me. Why don't you just say it? It's much more simple.

ARMAND. If I say it, it will not be today.

MARGUERITE. Never say it.

ARMAND. Why?

MARGUERITE. Because only two things can come of it. Either I shall not accept – then you will have a grudge against me – or I shall accept, and you will have a mistress who is sad or gay with a gaiety sadder than grief, who spits up blood and spends a hundred thousand francs a year. That is all very well for a rich old man like the Baron, but it is very bad for a young man like you.… If what you say is true, go away at once. Love me a little less or understand me a little better. I'm not worth much. You're too young and sensitive to live in a world like ours. Love some other woman and marry… I'm trying to be honest with you.

ARMAND. What if I were to tell you that I've spent whole nights beneath your windows and that for two months I've treasured a glove you dropped.

MARGUERITE. I should not believe you.

ARMAND. You're right to laugh at me. I'm a fool. There's nothing else to do but laugh at me.

MARGUERITE. Armand, can't we just be friends?

ARMAND. That's too much, and not enough. Don't you believe in love, Marguerite?

MARGUERITE. I don't know what it is. It's hard to believe in it if you've never had it.

ARMAND. *(crushing her in his embrace)* Let me make you believe. We'll rent a country house. Fresh air and good food will make you well in no time.

MARGUERITE. But that takes money.

ARMAND. I have money.

MARGUERITE. How much?

ARMAND. I have seven thousand francs a year.

MARGUERITE. *(pulling away from him and laughing)* I spend more than that in a week. And I've never been too particular where it came from, as I guess you know.

ARMAND. Don't talk like that!

MARGUERITE. It's true. The hard cold facts are we need hard cold cash. Why, the rental of a country house. horses, and a carriage to get around, to get us there and back…Enough for the table, even simple food costs money…No servants except for Nanine… *(handing him a pen and paper)* Oh, I'm no good at arithmetic. You figure it out.

(**ARMAND** *sits down at the desk and begins figuring. A knock at the door.* **NANINE** *enters with an enormous bouquet of red camellias.*)

NANINE. *(aside to* **MARGUERITE***)* The Baron de Varville sent these. Looks like he's learned his lesson. They're camellias this time.

ARMAND. *(finishing the sum)* Eighty thousand francs.

NANINE. He's waiting downstairs.

MARGUERITE. What did you say?

ARMAND. I said we'll need eighty thousand francs.

NANINE. I said the Baron de Varville is waiting downstairs.

ARMAND. But don't worry, darling, I'll get it somewhere.

MARGUERITE. Eighty thousand francs.

(**ARMAND** *tries to take* **MARGUERITE** *in his arms but she resists*)

Take this camellia and bring it back to me when it dies.

(She hands **ARMAND** *a flower and he kisses it.)*

ARMAND. When will that be?

MARGUERITE. How long does it take a flower to wither? A morning, an evening. Tomorrow night.

ARMAND. *(crushing the flower in his hand)* Here, it's dead already.

MARGUERITE. No, no, impossible. I wear red camellias when I've got the rag on…when the moon is not favorable to pleasure. I'll be wearing white ones tomorrow.

ARMAND. I can't wait. Let me sleep here tonight beside you like your brother or at the foot of your bed like your dog. But let me wait here until the camellias turn white.

MARGUERITE. You put tears on my hand. Yes. Yes. No! Yes!

ARMAND. *(overjoyed)* You'll take me? Like this, at a moment's notice?

MARGUERITE. Does it seem strange to you? *(taking his hand and placing it on her heart)* Feel my heart beating. I shall not live as long as others so I have promised myself to live more quickly.

ARMAND. Don't talk like that, I beg of you.

MARGUERITE. But however short a time I have to live, I shall yet live longer than your love.

ARMAND. I thought you didn't like sad thoughts.

MARGUERITE. I don't. But they come sometimes.

(Bell rings.)

NANINE. *(enters whispering)* Madame, the Baron is waiting. Shall I send him away?

MARGUERITE. *(aside to* **NANINE***)* Tell him to wait. *(to* **ARMAND***)* Armand, would you run out and get me some marrons glacés? I suddenly have the maddest craving for marrons glacés.

ARMAND. Aren't there any in the house?

MARGUERITE. No, and nothing but marrons glacés will do. Please go out and get me some.

ARMAND. Marguerite, is something wrong? I feel you're trying to get rid of me.

MARGUERITE. Now what on earth gave you that idea? Come back at midnight, and I'll be waiting for you.

ARMAND. How do I know you'll let me in when I come back?

MARGUERITE. *(giving him a key)* I'll give you the key and you can let yourself in. Now go, quickly.

(**ARMAND** *starts out the door.* **MARGUERITE** *blocks his way and shows him another)* No, this way.

(**ARMAND** *rushes out. There is a pause.* **ARMAND** *rushes in again.)*

ARMAND. I love you. *(exits)*

MARGUERITE. *(to* **NANINE**) Is it possible that he does love me? Or can I even be sure that I love him, I who have never loved? Show the Baron in, Nanine.

NANINE. I shall pray for you, Madame.

MARGUERITE. Why?

NANINE. Because you are in danger.

MARGUERITE. Oh pooh. Lying keeps my teeth white. Send the Baron in, Nanine.

(The **BARON** *enters.)*

Baron!

VARVILLE. You kept me waiting long enough.

MARGUERITE. Hello, you. I have just been putting my account books in order. *(showing him the book)* See?

VARVILLE. Lovely.

MARGUERITE. But, look at all these bills. I have eighty thousand francs' worth of debts. Will you lend me the money?

VARVILLE. No.

MARGUERITE. What will I do?

VARVILLE. Come with me to Siberia (**MARGUERITE** *coughs*) and I'll give you all the money you want.

MARGUERITE. If you are my friend, why won't you give it me now?

VARVILLE. Because if I do, you may no longer have any use for me. It has been months since we've as much as spent a night together.

(**VARVILLE** *plants a kiss on* **MARGUERITE***'s arm. Lipstick is left. She wipes it off and sprays it with an atomizer.*)

Until we do, your bills will go unpaid.

(**MARGUERITE** *sits down at the piano and begins to play Chopin.* **VARVILLE** *looks over the papers on the desk. He finds the sheet on which* **ARMAND** *was doing the sum and picks it up.*)

What's this? "House: thirty thousand francs; horses and carriage: twenty thousand... Nanine, Marguerite, and myself... thirty thousand... Who is this "myself"?

MARGUERITE. *(still playing)* Myself, of course. My doctor insists that I go to the country this summer for my health. That's why I asked you for the eighty thousand francs. I'm afraid of getting sick again. I know how it bores you.

VARVILLE. This note says, "Nanine, Marguerite, *and myself...*" A summer in the country, away from the glamour of Paris, living quietly with the cows and the chickens sounds very unlike you, my dear.

MARGUERITE. But, it's true.

VARVILLE. You can't fool me. I know you've found a playmate for this rustic holiday.

MARGUERITE. *(stops playing suddenly)* Damn Chopin and all his sharps and flats!

VARVILLE. I'm afraid your mind isn't on it, my dear.

MARGUERITE. You know quite well that I could never play it.

VARVILLE. Let me spend the night and you can have all the money you need.

MARGUERITE. Only if you will play the piano for me. *(rings for* **NANINE***)*

VARVILLE. *(bitterly)* My one merit. *(begins to play)*

MARGUERITE. *(aside to* **NANINE***)* Bolt the door and don't answer it, no matter what happens.

NANINE. Yes, Madame. *(exits)*

VARVILLE. Are you two through whispering over there?

MARGUERITE. I was just giving some orders to Nanine.

VARVILLE. Yes, I'm sure you were. *(Continues playing. The doorbell rings.)* Someday I'm going to get temperamental and complain when doorbells ring while I am trying to play.

MARGUERITE. *(pulling out whip and masks of black leather)* Did the doorbell ring? I didn't hear it.

VARVILLE. *(continuing to play)* Does my music shut out the world for you, my dear?

MARGUERITE. You play beautifully. *(puts on mask)*

VARVILLE. You lie beautifully.

MARGUERITE. *(masking* **VARVILLE***)* Thank you, that's more than I deserve.

VARVILLE. Oh, no, it's not half as much as you deserve. *(They laugh. Doorbell. The clock begins striking twelve.)* I wonder who it could be at this hour.

MARGUERITE. *(handcuffs* **VARVILLE** *to the piano and pulls a dildo out of the bag)* If I told you, you wouldn't believe me.

VARVILLE. Try me.

MARGUERITE. *(whipping him)* I could say that someone has found the wrong door. *(laughs)*

VARVILLE. *(laughing)* The wrong door! That's a good one!

MARGUERITE. Or I could say, it was the great love of my life.
VARVILLE. The great romance of your life! *(laughs)*
MARGUERITE. That might have been! *(starts to whip piano)*

(They both laugh – she ironically, he bitterly – as the curtain falls.)

ACT II

Scene One

(A country house at Auteuil. A room looking out on a garden.)

ARMAND. Where is Marguerite?

PRUDENCE. She is in the garden picking strawberries with Nichette, who has come to spend the day with her. I'm just going to join them.

ARMAND. One moment, Prudence. A week ago, Marguerite gave you some diamond bracelets to have reset. What has become of them?

PRUDENCE. Well, that's a long story. I…er…I…ah…

ARMAND. Come, tell me frankly. Where are Marguerite's bracelets?

PRUDENCE. Do you want the truth?

ARMAND. Of course I want the truth.

PRUDENCE. Sold.

ARMAND. Her gowns?

PRUDENCE. Sold.

ARMAND. Her horses and her jewels?

PRUDENCE. Sold and pawned.

ARMAND. Who has sold and pawned them?

PRUDENCE. I did.

ARMAND. Why did you not tell me?

PRUDENCE. Marguerite made me promise not to.

ARMAND. And where has all the money gone?

PRUDENCE. In payments. Ah, my dear fellow, she didn't want to tell you. Marguerite's creditors went to the Baron de Varville to settle, and he had them thrown out of his house. They wanted their money. I gave them part payment out of the few thousand francs you gave me. But, someone told them that Marguerite had been abandoned by the Baron and was living with a penniless young man. They stormed her house and ripped off all of her goods. Marguerite wanted to sell everything, but it was too late. So rather than ask you for the money, she sold her horses, her carriage, her gowns, and her jewels. Here are the receipts and the pawn tickets. *(gives him the receipts)*

ARMAND. How much money is needed?

PRUDENCE. Fifty thousand francs. Ah, I hate to say I told you so. You think it is enough to be in love, and go to the country, and live on air. You'll soon find out that someone has to pay the rent on your pastoral dream! Ah, l'amour, l'amour. Toujours l'amour! Yecch.

ARMAND. Ask our creditors for a fortnight's grace. I will pay.

PRUDENCE. Are you going to borrow the money?

ARMAND. Yes. I suspected something of the kind and have written to my solicitor.

PRUDENCE. No, Armand, you'll only quarrel with your father and ruin your whole future.

ARMAND. Hush, she's coming.

(MARGUERITE enters wearing wooden shoes.)

I want you to scold Prudence for me, dearest!

MARGUERITE. Why?

ARMAND. She forgot to bring me my mail, so I shall have to go to Paris to get it myself. I didn't give anyone our address here because I wanted to be left in peace. I'll be gone only a couple of hours.

MARGUERITE. Yes, go dear, but do come back quickly.

ARMAND. I shall drive in and be back in an hour.

MARGUERITE. And take care of yourself.

ARMAND. And you too. Take care of her, Prudence.

MARGUERITE. Each moment will be an eternity.

PRUDENCE. For God's sake, he's not going to war! He's just going to get his mail.

NICHETTE. *(entering)* Oh, what a happy couple!

ARMAND. Hello, Nichette. I'm just leaving. I'm sure you girls have a lot to talk over. *(exit with* **PRUDENCE***)*

MARGUERITE. You see, this is where we have been living for the last three months. Salon, bedroom, anteroom, and kitchen. Furnished in a way that would divert a hypochondriac. Was I right?

NICHETTE. Are you happy?

MARGUERITE. Very happy.

(Picks up hand bell, rings it with abandon. **NANINE** *enters with tea on a serving tray.)*

NICHETTE. I always told you, Marguerite, that this was the way to be happy. Many a time Gustave and I have said to each other, "When will Marguerite really love someone and settle down?"

MARGUERITE. Well, your wish is fulfilled. I am really in love. I think it was watching you and Gustave that first made me envious.

NICHETTE. We have two dear little rooms in the rue Blanche.

MARGUERITE. Two little rooms.

NICHETTE. And Gustave says that I am not to work and he will buy me a carriage, one of these days.

MARGUERITE. One of these days!

NICHETTE. And we're going to get married, too.

MARGUERITE. One of these days?

NICHETTE. Soon.

MARGUERITE. You will be very happy. *(***MARGUERITE** *pours tea.)* Sugar?

*(***MARGUERITE** *places twelve sugar cubes in her cup, one by one, hesitates with the thirteenth, decides against it.)*

NICHETTE. But aren't you going to get married and do as we do?

MARGUERITE. Whom should I marry?

NICHETTE. Why, Armand, of course!

MARGUERITE. Armand would marry me tomorrow if I wished it. But I love him too much for that.

NICHETTE. But so long as you are happy, what does it matter?

MARGUERITE. I *am* happy. I can tell you because I know you will understand. *(takes off wooden shoes)* The Marguerite that used to be and the Marguerite of today are two different beings. I used to spend enough money on camellias to keep a poor family for a year.

(NANINE enters with a dish of strawberries.)

But, now, a flower like this that Armand gave me this morning is enough to fill my whole day with perfume. What do you call this flower, Nanine?

NANINE. Bittersweet. *(exits)*

MARGUERITE. And yet money-money-money-money. It was the Baron de Varville who paid for everything. Now I'm in debt. Why can't anything ever be perfect?

NICHETTE. If only you could be content with two little rooms like ours.

MARGUERITE. Listen, Nichette. I came up from grinding poverty and it stinks. I never want to go back to work in a shop and live in two little rooms with cucarachas and ratónes. No, no, I'll never go back! There are only two ways a woman may rise from the gutter and become a queen: prostitution or the stage. And, believe me, Nichette, I'd rather peddle my coosie in the streets than become an actress!

NICHETTE. There is another way a woman may rise, Marguerite. A woman may marry.

MARGUERITE. Marriage is nothing but legalized prostitution. *(Salutes with fist. Throws a strawberry up and catches it in her mouth.)*

NICHETTE. I think you're wrong, Marguerite, terribly wrong.

MARGUERITE. Perhaps…perhaps…

NICHETTE. If only you would come to visit our two little rooms, I'm sure you would change your mind.

MARGUERITE. Perhaps I will…one of these days.

NANINE. *(entering)* There is a gentleman here who wishes to speak to you Madame.

MARGUERITE. That will be my lawyer. I was expecting him. *(to* **NICHETTE***)* Please excuse me.

NICHETTE. I really must be going. I want to have Gustave's dinner ready for him when he gets home from the office.

MARGUERITE. Cooking? Sister, have you no pride?

NICHETTE. Pride? That's one luxury a woman in love can't afford. Toodle-oo, Marguerite!

MARGUERITE. Ta-ta, Nichette!

(Exit **NICHETTE.** *Enter* **PRUDENCE.***)*

PRUDENCE. I've sold your diamond earrings. Here's your receipt. Here are the earrings. *(pulling earrings from* **MARGUERITE***'s ears)* Here's my commission. I'm off! Good-bye, Marguerite. You know where to find me if you need me. L'amour, l'amour. *(exits)*

DUVAL. *(entering)* Mademoiselle Marguerite Gautier?

MARGUERITE. Yes, I am she. To whom do I have the honor of speaking?

DUVAL. To Monsieur Duval.

MARGUERITE. Monsieur Duval?

DUVAL. Yes, Madame, I am Armand's father. Is Armand here?

MARGUERITE. *(troubled)* No, Armand is often here. But just now he is away, at Paris.

DUVAL. Good. I want to speak to you alone. You see, I know what's going on here. My son is ruining himself for you.

MARGUERITE. You are mistaken, sir. I accept nothing from Armand.

DUVAL. Am I to understand, then, as your habits of luxury are well known, that my son is mean enough to help you spend what you receive from others?

MARGUERITE. You must excuse me, sir. Your manner of addressing me is not what I should have expected from a gentleman. I must ask your permission to withdraw.

DUVAL. Your indignation is cleverly assumed, Madame. They were right when they told me you were dangerous.

MARGUERITE. Dangerous to myself, perhaps, but not to others.

DUVAL. Then will you explain to me the meaning of this letter? It is from my lawyer informing me that my son wishes to turn over to you the inheritance he received from his mother.

MARGUERITE. I assure you that, if Armand has done such a thing, it is entirely without my knowledge. He knew that, if he had offered it to me, I should have refused it.

DUVAL. That was not always your method, I think.

MARGUERITE. It is true, now...

DUVAL. Now?

MARGUERITE. Now I have learned what true love means.

DUVAL. Fine phrases, Madame.

MARGUERITE. You force me to disclose to you that which I should have preferred to keep secret. Ever since I knew and loved your son, I have been selling my horses, my carriage, my gowns, and my jewels. A moment ago, when I was told that someone wished to speak with me, I concluded that it was in connection with the sale of furniture, pictures, and the rest of the luxury with which you have reproached me. I was not expecting you, sir, so you may be quite sure that this paper was not prepared especially for you, but if you doubt what I say, read this.... (*Gives him the bill of sale which* **PRUDENCE** *has drawn up.*)

DUVAL. (*reading*) A bill of sale on your jewels, the purchaser to pay your creditors, the balance to be given to you? (*looks at her in astonishment*) Have I been mistaken?

MARGUERITE. You have. It is Armand who changed me.

DUVAL. Forgive me, Madame, for my discourtesy a moment ago. I was not acquainted with you and quite unprepared for what I was to find. I was deeply hurt by my son's silence and ingratitude of which I judged you to be the cause. I beg your pardon.

MARGUERITE. Thank you.

(pause)

DUVAL. And what if I ask you to give Armand a greater proof of your love?

MARGUERITE. No! No! You are going to ask something terrible of me. I knew I was too happy.

DUVAL. Let us speak together now like two friends.

MARGUERITE. Yes...friends.

DUVAL. I speak to you as a father who asks you for the happiness of his two children.

MARGUERITE. Of his two children?

DUVAL. Yes, Marguerite, of his two children. I have a daughter, young, beautiful, pure.

(**MARGUERITE** *reacts, realizing he's not talking about her*)

She is to be married and she, too, has made her love the dream of her life. Society is exacting in certain respects, especially provincial society. The family of my future son-in-law have learned of the manner in which Armand is living; they have given me to understand that the marriage cannot take place if it continues. Marguerite, in the name of your love, grant me the happiness of my child.

MARGUERITE. How can I refuse what you ask with so much gentleness and consideration? I understand. You are right. I will go back to Paris. I will leave Armand for a while. Besides, the joy of our reunion will help us to forger the pain of parting.

DUVAL. Thank you, Marguerite, thank you, but there is still something that I must ask of you.

MARGUERITE. Can you ask anything more of me?

DUVAL. A temporary parting is not enough.

MARGUERITE. You mean you want me to leave Armand altogether?

DUVAL. You must.

MARGUERITE. Never! You don't know how we love each other.

DUVAL. My son is as dear to me as he can possibly be to you.

MARGUERITE. But you have friends and a family. I have only Armand. I'm ill. I have only a few years to live. To leave Armand would kill me.

DUVAL. Come, come, let's not exaggerate. You're not going to die. What you feel is the melancholy of happiness, knowing that even love can't last forever. No woman is worthy of a man if she lets him ruin himself. Think of Armand's career. He will never go through doors you cannot go through. He can't present you to his family and friends. You're killing his right to a normal life.

MARGUERITE. You're not telling me anything I haven't said to myself a hundred times – but I never let myself go through to the end. *(to herself)* A woman once she has fallen can never rise again. *(to **DUVAL**)* But a man can go back he can always go back!

DUVAL. What career would remain open to him? What will be left to you both when you are old? Who can promise that he will not be less dazzled when time casts the first shadow over your beauty? Has not your own experience taught you that the human heart cannot be trusted?

MARGUERITE. My God!

DUVAL. No unprotected woman can afford to waste the best years of her life. What will your old age be, doubly deserted, doubly desolate?

MARGUERITE. What must I do? Tell me.

DUVAL. *You* must tell Armand that you no longer love him.

MARGUERITE. He won't believe me.

DUVAL. Leave him.

MARGUERITE. He will follow me.

DUVAL. In that case...

MARGUERITE. *Do* you believe that I love Armand with a love that is truly unselfish?

DUVAL. Yes, Marguerite.

MARGUERITE. Then, sir, will you kiss me just once, as you would your own daughter? And believe me when I tell you it is the only really pure kiss that I have ever received. And promise me that one day you will tell this beautiful and pure young girl that somewhere in the world there is a woman, who had only one thought, one hope, one dream in life, and that for her sake she renounced them all *(throws spray of bittersweet off)* and that she died of it. Because I shall die of it and then, perhaps, God will forgive me.

DUVAL. *(moved in spite of himself)* Poor girl! *(kisses her)*

MARGUERITE. I swear that he shall never know what has passed between us. One last favor.

DUVAL. Ask it.

MARGUERITE. Within a few hours, Armand will experience one of the greatest sorrows he has ever known, or perhaps ever will know. He will need someone who loves him. Will you be here, sir, at his side?

DUVAL. What are you going to do?

MARGUERITE. If I told you, it would be your duty to prevent it.

DUVAL. You are a noble girl. But I am afraid.

MARGUERITE. Fear nothing, sir. He shall hate me. *(rings for* **NANINE***)*

DUVAL. I shall never forget what I and my family owe you.

MARGUERITE. Make no mistake, monsieur, whatever I do is not for you. Everything I do is for Armand.

DUVAL. Is there nothing I can do for you in acknowledgment of the debt that I shall owe you?

MARGUERITE. When I am dead and Armand curses my memory, tell him that I loved him and that I proved it. We shall never meet again. Good-bye.

(*Exit* **DUVAL.** **MARGUERITE** *alone.*)

Venus Castina give me strength. (*writes a letter*)

NANINE. (*entering all smiles*) You rang for me, Madame?

MARGUERITE. (*weeping*) Yes, there is something I want you to do for me.

NANINE. What is it?

MARGUERITE. Take this letter, Nanine.

NANINE. Why, you're weeping. I don't know what's in it, but I can see that the thought of it makes your blood run cold.

MARGUERITE. Read the address.

NANINE. The Baron de Var…Now what do you want to send this for? I thought you were so happy with Monsieur Duval.

MARGUERITE. I was.

NANINE. Then what are you doing, you foolish girl?

MARGUERITE. I'm going to make my love hate me, Nanine. Make him hate me! Make him hate me! (*sobs*)

NANINE. But…

MARGUERITE. Hush. Go at once! (*exit* **NANINE**) And now for Armand. (*begins writing a second letter*)

ARMAND. (*entering*) Ah, Marguerite, I'm back.

MARGUERITE. Already?

ARMAND. What's the matter? You don't seem glad to see me.

MARGUERITE. I saw you this morning and last night and yesterday and the day before that.

ARMAND. How was your day?

MARGUERITE. Well, this morning Prudence and I walked down the road to see the new cow. And this afternoon, I washed my hair. Those were the two big events of my day.

ARMAND. You seem so strange. What's the matter?

MARGUERITE. I'm bored.

ARMAND. Bored? But this morning you said you liked the country.

MARGUERITE. That was this morning.

ARMAND. Are things so different now?

MARGUERITE. Yes, things are different now. This is no life for me.

ARMAND. What does this mean?

MARGUERITE. I'm going back to Paris.

ARMAND. But you said it would kill you if you went back to Paris.

MARGUERITE. Perhaps it will. If I'm going to die, I'd rather die gaily than of boredom. Wasn't one summer all you wanted, dahling?

ARMAND. I won't let you go. *(He takes her in his arms and holds her very tight)*

MARGUERITE. You must let me go, Armand. You must. It's better this way, better for both of us.

ARMAND. You've put tears on my hand.

MARGUERITE. I had to cry a little. There, I'm better now. Believe me, I've loved you as long as I can. It's not my fault that I can't love you forever. We don't make our own hearts, Armand.

ARMAND. *(releasing her)* No, Marguerite, you can't help it that you can love me only a little while. Just as I can't help it that I will love you for the rest of my life.

MARGUERITE. *(bitterly)* That's the way it is. I'm going.

ARMAND. I can't let you go!

MARGUERITE. You must. The Baron de Varville is expecting me.

ARMAND. The Baron de Varville?!! I could kill you for this.

MARGUERITE. I'm not worth killing. You can't give me the things in life I want. I can't part with my horses, my carriage, my gowns, and my jewels. I thought I could, but I can't.

ARMAND. You filthy slut!

*(**MARGUERITE** runs out the door. Calling after her)*

Marguerite, forgive me! I didn't mean it! Marguerite, don't leave me! Please don't leave me!

*(**DUVAL SR.** has entered at the back. **ARMAND** turns, sees his father, and collapses into his arms in tears.)*

Father!

Scene Two

(A soirée at Olympe's house in Paris, six months later.)

PRUDENCE. What a wonderful party!

GASTON. Yes, splendid, splendid. I've been losing all my money.

PRUDENCE. That's all right. Gambling is a gentleman's vice.

GASTON. Olympe has outdone herself tonight. This is the most extravagant soirée of the season.

PRUDENCE. I wonder if Saint Gaudens knows what it is costing him.

OLYMPE. *(overhearing)* His wife does!

PRUDENCE. Very witty!

GASTON. What a charming gown you are wearing tonight, Olympe.

OLYMPE. Thank you. It's from Prudence's shop. A Duvernoy original. I wanted to wear a gown by Gongora, but Saint Gaudens wouldn't hear of it.

SAINT GAUDENS. My dear, it wasn't you. A grande bateau-mouche tricked out in Punch and Judy orchids. Foh!

OLYMPE. Whenever Saint Gaudens doesn't like the dress I'm wearing, I take it off!

SAINT GAUDENS. Gaston, do you think a demimondaine such as this one might want to give up her former life and lead a simple and pure existence?

GASTON. Put a duck on a lake among swans and you will observe that the duck misses its mire and will return to it.

SAINT GAUDENS. Homesick for the mud. Then you don't believe in repentant Magdalenes.

GASTON. I do. In the desert!

OLYMPE. I like poise, don't you? I always insist upon it. For instance, a woman should always leave a man before he leaves her.

PRUDENCE. And here I am, six months later, and still in the same dress.

OLYMPE. Fermez la bouche. Nobody's going to buy you a new one.

BUTLER. *(announcing)* Monsieur Armand Duval.

GASTON. Look, there's Armand.

SAINT GAUDENS. Hurumph!

GASTON. But where is Marguerite?

OLYMPE. *(mit schadenfreude)* Haven't you heard? They've broken up!

GASTON. Impossible.

PRUDENCE. It's quite true. It happened last summer at Auteuil.

GASTON. Then they've really parted. Will Marguerite be here tonight?

PRUDENCE. No, not a chance.

OLYMPE. Don't be too sure, Prudence. I invited the Baron de Varville.

GASTON. Then Varville won her after all.

OLYMPE. "Bought" is more the word, I should say.

SAINT GAUDENS. Don't be a camp, Olympe.

OLYMPE. How can you reproach me? I've been a very good friend to Marguerite. Didn't I buy her horses, her carriage, her gowns, and her jewels when she needed the money?

PRUDENCE. It is true.

OLYMPE. *(pointing out various items of jewelry she is wearing)* See, these and this one and this one. I got them for peanuts. Even this gown belonged to her.

PRUDENCE. The Baron has given her back everything that she lost – her horses, her carriage, her gowns, and her jewels. Ah, l'amour, l'amour! For what happiness is worth in this world, she is happy. But she never sleeps.

OLYMPE. She goes everywhere: theaters, balls, orgies, and operas.

PRUDENCE. She won't listen to her doctor. She won't last long at this rate. Ah, l'amour, l'amour, toujours l'amour!

GASTON. *(greeting* **ARMAND***)* Well, Armand, what a surprise to see you. I thought you'd left Paris.

ARMAND. Well, you were wrong.

GASTON. I hear you've broken with Marguerite.

ARMAND. You heard right.

GASTON. Do you ever see her?

ARMAND. No, never.

GASTON. I hear she is coming here tonight.

ARMAND. *(starts)* Then I *shall* see her.

GASTON. Of course, she'll be with Varville.

ARMAND. So much the better. *(intensely)* Listen, Gaston, I'm going crazy. Ever since Marguerite left me, I have hardly slept. And when I do sleep, I have nightmares.

GASTON. Dear boy.

ARMAND. I came here tonight because I knew she would be here. I want to punish her for leaving me.

GASTON. Armand, be careful. She is a woman, and any act of revenge on your part will seem like cowardice.

ARMAND. Then let her escort protect her. I would give anything for an excuse to kill him.

BUTLER. Madame Marguerite Gautier. The Baron de Varville.

(**ARMAND** *goes over and puts his arm around* **OLYMPE**, *who plays up to him.* **MARGUERITE** *enters wearing the same gown as* **OLYMPE** *but much more fabulous. There is a momentary confrontation between the two women.)*

MARGUERITE. *(to* **VARVILLE***)* I don't feel well. I want to go home.

OLYMPE. *(turning on* **PRUDENCE**, *furiously)* I thought you said this gown was an original!

PRUDENCE. *(sheepishly)* Well, it was. The first time I made it.

OLYMPE. *(wringing* **PRUDENCE**'s *neck)* You treacherous old harridan! *(spinning around furiously)* I won't be outdone in my own home!

(During her tantrum, her dress becomes disheveled and one tit is exposed; she hides it with her fan. Regaining her composure, she faces **MARGUERITE**.*)*

You made me lose my poise and for this, I shall never forgive you! *(starts out)*

SAINT GAUDENS. Where are you going?

OLYMPE. I'm going to change into my Gongora with the Punch and Judy orchids! *(exits)*

MARGUERITE. Please, Varville, I want to go home. I'm ill.

VARVILLE. Your illness bores me, my dear.

*(***MARGUERITE** *drops her fan.)*

You've dropped your fan.

MARGUERITE. What?

VARVILLE. You've dropped your fan.

MARGUERITE. Oh, have I? *(bends over and picks it up)*

GASTON. Good evening, Marguerite.

MARGUERITE. *(drying her eyes)* Good evening, dear Gaston, I'm so glad to see you.

GASTON. You're weeping. What is the matter?

MARGUERITE. It's nothing. I'm just unhappy, that's all.

GASTON. What are you doing here?

MARGUERITE. I am not my own mistress. Besides, I do all I can to forget.

GASTON. Take my advice and leave at once! I fear there may be some trouble between Armand and the Baron, perhaps a duel.

MARGUERITE. A duel between Armand and Varville?

GASTON. Make some excuse. Say you are ill.

MARGUERITE. You are right. *(to* **VARVILLE**, *who has been cruising the* **BUTLER***)* Varville, I'm terribly ill. We must leave at once.

VARVILLE. We're staying right where we are. I'm not missing the best soirée of the season because of Armand Duval.

(**OLYMPE** *enters in an outrageous Gongora gown with Punch and Judy orchids.*)

GASTON. Is this a woman or a circus tent? *(pops one of the balloons that hold up her skirt)*

OLYMPE. You stop that. *(hanging around* **ARMAND***'s neck and talking in baby talk)* Look, Armand's been winning at cards.

ARMAND. Yes, I'm testing the old saying, "Lucky at cards, unlucky in love."

OLYMPE. How do you like me, Armand?

ARMAND. I like you as well as you like my money.

OLYMPE. Come, let's greet the Baron de Varville and Marguerite Gautier together.

ARMAND. I will on one condition.

OLYMPE. I'll do anything as long as it's *not* within reason.

ARMAND. *(imitating baby talk)* If you don't stop talking like that, I'm going to knock your teeth down your throat! I want you to insult Marguerite.

OLYMPE. I'd be delighted.

(**ARMAND** *and* **OLYMPE**, *petting each other, go to greet the* **BARON** *and* **MARGUERITE**.)

Good evening, Marrrrrrrrrrrguerrrrrritttttte, Baron.

MARGUERITE. Good evening, Olym*p*e. *(She spits the final "p" in Olympe.)*

ARMAND. Marguerite, Baro*n*. *(bows)*

VARVILLE. Good evening. *(bows stiffly)*

MARGUERITE. Good evening.

VARVILLE. We've just come from the Opera, where we heard Berenice Blowell.

OLYMPE. What did she sing?

VARVILLE. *Manon Lescaut.*

ARMAND. Ah, yes, *Manon Lescaut,* the story of a vile woman incapable of loyalty, who sold her young lover for an old man's gold.

OLYMPE. How very unoriginal. And most untrue. Women never betray their lovers.

ARMAND. Some do.

OLYMPE. Of course, but there are lovers and lovers.

ARMAND. Just as there are women and women.

(**MARGUERITE** *drops her fan again.*)

VARVILLE. You dropped your fan again, my dear.

(**ARMAND**, *intercepting* **MARGUERITE**, *picks up the fan and returns it to her.*)

MARGUERITE. Thank you.

ARMAND. Any gentleman would do the same.

(**VARVILLE** *makes a threatening movement toward* **ARMAND**, **MARGUERITE** *and* **OLYMPE** *draw the two men apart.*)

GASTON. Armand, would you care for a hand of baccarat?

ARMAND. Yes, I intend to make my fortune tonight. Then when I am really rich, I intend to go and live in the country.

OLYMPE. Alone?

ARMAND. No, with someone who went with me once before and left me. It all depends on how much I win. If I am wealthy, perhaps I can buy her back.

GASTON. Be quiet, Armand. Look at that poor girl.

ARMAND. It's an amusing story. You would enjoy it. There is an old buffoon who makes his appearance right at the very end – a sort of deus ex machina….

VARVILLE. Sir!

MARGUERITE. *(aside to* **VARVILLE***)* If you challenge Monsieur Duval to a duel, you will never see me again as long as you live.

ARMAND. You addressed yourself to me, sir?

VARVILLE. I did. Your luck tonight tempts me to try my own. I understand perfectly how you intend to use your winnings and I should be happy to help you increase them. Therefore, I propose to bet against you.

ARMAND. I accept with all my heart, sir. But remember, the reverse of the old saying may also be true. "Lucky in love, unlucky at cards."

(**ARMAND** *and* **VARVILLE** *begin gambling.*)

MARGUERITE. My God, what are they doing?

PRUDENCE. *(aside to* **BUTLER***)* Say dinner is served.

BUTLER. I beg your pardon?

PRUDENCE. Say dinner is served. *(gives him a good swift kick in the hams)*

BUTLER. *(blurts out)* Dinner is served!

PRUDENCE. Thank heavens! I'm famished. Dinner is ready, everyone. Come into the next room and eat! *(She herds everyone out.)* Ah, l'amour, l'amour!

MARGUERITE. Gaston, dahling, please ask Armand to come in here a moment. I must speak to him.

GASTON. I will. *(exits)*

VARVILLE. *(to* **MARGUERITE***)* Are you coming, my dear?

MARGUERITE. Go ahead without me. I need a moment to repair my maquillage.

VARVILLE. All right. But if you are longer than five minutes, I'll come back for you. *(exits)*

ARMAND. *(entering)* You sent for me?

MARGUERITE. Yes, Armand, I want to speak to you.

ARMAND. What do you want?

MARGUERITE. I want to beg you to please stop this.

ARMAND. Stop what?

MARGUERITE. This torture. I can't bear it.

ARMAND. I'm sure I don't know what you mean.

MARGUERITE. You do know what I mean. This continuous punishment. I can't bear it. I can't bear it.

ARMAND. What business is it of yours what I do? We mean nothing to each other anymore.

MARGUERITE. That's not true, Armand. I love you. I have always loved you.

ARMAND. Then come away with me at once!

MARGUERITE. Oh, I would give my life for one hour of such happiness, but it's impossible.

ARMAND. It will be humiliating for me, but I will do anything to have you back. You can take everything I own. You name your price.

MARGUERITE. Armand, stop!

ARMAND. *(on his knees)* Please, Marguerite. Since I have loved you, I can love no other. Help me! Help me!

MARGUERITE. I can't, Armand. I have promised not to.

ARMAND. Who have you promised?

MARGUERITE. Someone to whom I owe all the respect in the world.

ARMAND. *(incensed)* The Baron de Varville?

MARGUERITE. *(lying)* Yes.

*(***ARMAND*** throws open the doors to the next room.)*

ARMAND. Come in here, all of you. I have an announcement to make!

MARGUERITE. What are you doing?

(All enter, puzzled.)

ARMAND. You see this woman?

ALL. *(pointing simultaneously to* **MARGUERITE***)* Marguerite Gautier?

ARMAND. Yes, Marguerite Gautier! She spent a summer in the country with me once. I gave her everything I had. I loved her as I have never loved anyone and as I shall never love again. But that love was not enough for her. It meant less to her than horses, a carriage, and the diamonds around her neck. I have not yet paid her for the summer we spent together. You are my witnesses. I owe this woman nothing.

*(***ARMAND*** slaps* ***MARGUERITE*** *across the face with the bundle of franc notes he won and throws them at her.*

They fall about her in a flurry.)

VARVILLE. *(to* **ARMAND***)* Congratulations, young man. You have treated her as she deserved.

*(***ARMAND** *slaps* **VARVILLE** *across the face.* **MARGUERITE** *faints. Curtain.)*

ACT III

(MARGUERITE's bedroom. Paris, six months later. New Year's Day.)

(The light of dawn reveals snow falling outside the window of MARGUERITE's apartment. MARGUERITE is in bed asleep; NANINE has fallen asleep in a chair. GASTON enters [wearing a skeleton's head on the back of his head]. The occasional sound of a last reveler tooting his party horn is heard off stage along with a cry of "Happy New Year" and a snatch of "Auld Lang Syne" sung drunkenly. A bit of confetti might blow past the window. GASTON wears a party hat with bits of confetti in his hair and a few serpentines around his neck. He may be a little drunk on champagne, but not unbecomingly so.)

GASTON. She is still asleep. What time is it? Seven o'clock. Not yet daylight.

(The sound of loud snoring from NANINE.)

Faithful old Nanine. *(lights candle)* It is better to light one candle than to curse the darkness. *(He picks up MARGUERITE's purse from the mantel.)* Here's her purse. *(looking inside)* Empty! *(He reaches deep inside his pockets and pulls out some franc notes, turning his pockets inside out in the process.)*

MARGUERITE. *(waking)* I'm thirsty, Nanine.

GASTON. *(giving her some tea)* Here you are, old girl.

MARGUERITE. I'm cold. Nanine, throw another faggot on the fire!

NANINE. *(waking)* There are no more faggots in the house. *(falls asleep)*

MARGUERITE. *(plaintively looking out at the audience)* No faggots in the house? Open the window, Nanine. See if there are any in the street. *(seeing* **GASTON***)* Gaston, what are you doing here?

GASTON. Drink this first, and then I'll tell you. I am a born nurse.

MARGUERITE. But where is Nanine?

GASTON. Asleep. How do you feel this morning?

MARGUERITE. Better, Gaston dear. But why should you tire yourself like this?

GASTON. Tire myself? Nonsense! I've been out all night partying. I just wanted to wish you a Happy New Year.

MARGUERITE. New Year?

GASTON. I wanted to bring you flowers. But I couldn't find a single camellia in Paris. It seems there was a killing frost last night in the flower market.

MARGUERITE. I'm cold.

GASTON. Drink this.

MARGUERITE. It's strange that you should come here to take care of me. I always thought that you were just a scatterbrain who cared for nothing but pleasure.

GASTON. You were quite right.

*(***MARGUERITE*** laughs and then coughs.)*

Now, I'll tell you what we'll do.

MARGUERITE. What?

GASTON. You must try to sleep a little longer. There will be plenty of sunshine in the early part of the afternoon. Wrap yourself up well, and I will come back and take you for a drive. And then who'll sleep tonight?... Marguerite! Now I must go and call on my mother, and God knows what kind of a reception I'll get. I haven't been to see her in over a fortnight. I shall lunch with her and then call for you at one o'clock. How will that suit you?

MARGUERITE. I shall try to have enough strength.

GASTON. You will. Of course, you will. *(to* **NANINE**) Marguerite is awake. Until this afternoon then. *(exits)*

MARGUERITE. Until this afternoon. Are you tired, my poor old Nanine?

NANINE. A little. Madame.

MARGUERITE. Open the window, Nanine, and let in the morning air. I should like to get up.

NANINE. The doctor said you weren't to get out of bed.

MARGUERITE. Dear doctor. Always giving me good advice.

NANINE. He's going to have you well by spring.

MARGUERITE. When God said it was a sin to tell lies, he must have made an exception for doctors. I suppose they have a special dispensation from the pope every time they visit a patient. What have you got there?

NANINE. Presents, Madame.

MARGUERITE. Oh, yes, it's New Year's Day. How much can happen in a year!...A year ago today, we were sitting around the table singing and laughing....Where are the days, Nanine, when we still laughed? *(opens parcels)* A *ring* with a card from Saint Gaudens. A *bracelet!* From the Baron de Varville. He sent it all the way from Siberia. It's cold. What would he say if he could see me like this?...And marrons glacés! Well, men are not so forgetful, after all. Joseph has a little niece, hasn't he, Nanine?

NANINE. Yes, Madame.

MARGUERITE. Give him these marrons glacés, for the little girl. It's been a long time since I've wanted any. Is that all?

NANINE. There is a letter.

MARGUERITE. A letter! *(takes letter, opens it, reads)* "My dearest Marguerite I have called again and again, but was not allowed to see you. I cannot bear the thought that you will have no share in the happiest day of my life. I am to be married on the first of January. It is the New Year's gift that Gustave was keeping as a surprise for me. I do hope that you will be able to come to my wedding – such a simple, quiet wedding in the Chapel of Sainte Thérèse in the Madeleine. I kiss you, dear, with all the fervor of my most happy heart. Toodle-oo. Nichette." And so, there is happiness for everyone in the world except for me. But there, I am ungrateful. Please, shut the window, I'm cold. *(The bell rings.)* Ah, there is the bell. See who it is, Nanine.

NANINE. *(coming back)* Madame Duvernoy would like to see you.

MARGUERITE. Let her come in. Pretty please, let her in. Just this once. *(Etc.* **NANINE** *relents.)* There's the good Nanine.

PRUDENCE. *(entering)* Well, my dear Marguerite, how are you this morning?

MARGUERITE. Better, thank you, Prudence. And how are you?

PRUDENCE. Rotten, thank you. I drank too much champagne last night at Olympe's and I've got the worst hangover. My stomach, oh my God, I don' know when I've had such indigestion. Olympe has a new chef who is a genius an absolute artist of genius. But he's ruined my stomach. And then, there's a headache to top it all off. And my sciatica has been acting up again. I'm feeling terrible. I'm really enjoying very poor health.

MARGUERITE. I'm sorry to hear it.

PRUDENCE. Have you heard? The Baron de Varville has recovered from the duel. Fortunately, it was only a scratch and Armand can return from exile. The Baron has taken up with little boys. He likes to get kicked in the rump by little boys! All that money he used to spend on jewels is now being wasted on toys Ah, l'amour, l'amour! Send Nanine away for a moment. I want to speak to you alone.

MARGUERITE. You can finish the other room first, Nanine. I'll call you if I need you.

(exit **NANINE***)*

PRUDENCE. I wonder if you would do me a favor, Marguerite?

MARGUERITE. What is it?

PRUDENCE. You have money in hand, don't you?

MARGUERITE. You know that I have been very short of money for some time

PRUDENCE. It's New Year's Day and I have some presents to buy. I'm badly in need of two hundred francs. Do you think you could lend it to me until the end of the month?

MARGUERITE. Until the end of the month!

PRUDENCE. If it's not inconvenient.

MARGUERITE. Well, I do rather need what money I have left.

PRUDENCE. *(in a snit)* Very well, then, we'll say no more about it. *(pause)* I didn't want to mention it, but you do owe me two hundred francs for the bonnet I made for you last Easter.

MARGUERITE. Bonnet?

PRUDENCE. Of course, it was violet voile with Costa Rica roses. Don't tell me you've forgotten it.

MARGUERITE. How could I forget the Costa Rica roses.

PRUDENCE. Why, here's your purse.

MARGUERITE. It's empty.

PRUDENCE. *(looking inside the purse)* Nonsense! It's full of money!

MARGUERITE. Full of money?...Gaston! How much is there?

PRUDENCE. Five hundred francs!

MARGUERITE. Then take the two hundred that you need.

PRUDENCE. Are you sure the rest will be enough for you?

MARGUERITE. I shall have all I need. Don't worry about me.

PRUDENCE. You are looking better this morning.

MARGUERITE. I feel better.

PRUDENCE. It won't be long now before spring will be here. Warm weather and a little country air will soon put you right.

MARGUERITE. Yes, that's what I need.

PRUDENCE. *(going out)* Well, good-bye, dear. And thank you again.

MARGUERITE. Send Nanine to me.

(enter NANINE*)*

NANINE. Has she been asking you for money again?

MARGUERITE. Yes.

NANINE. Did you give it to her?

MARGUERITE. Money is such a little thing to give, and she needed it badly, she said. But we need some too, don't we? We must buy some New Year's presents. Take this bracelet that has just come. Sell it and come back as quickly as you can.

NANINE. But what about you?

MARGUERITE. I shall not need anything. Oh, Nanine. Sweet Nanine. Perfect Nanine. You will not be gone very long. You know the way to the pawnbroker's. He's bought enough from me these last three months.

(Exit NANINE. JOSEPH *has been standing in the background listening.)*

BUTLER. *(coming forward)* Excuse me, Madame, I am a man of few words. Nanine and I have put away a little money for our old age. It isn't much. But it might be enough for a pilgrimage to Lourdes. Please accept our life's savings.

MARGUERITE. Yes, it is a miracle that I need. Thank you, Joseph. But there is only one miracle that can save me...Armand's return.

NANINE. *(entering)* Here is the money, Madame. I had to smuggle it past the bailiff waiting downstairs.

MARGUERITE. *(putting the money into an envelope with a note)* Take this to Nichette at the Chapel of Sainte Thérèse in the Madeleine. Tell her not to open it until after the wedding.

BUTLER. Yes, Madame. *(exit with* NANINE*)*

MARGUERITE. If only I had some word from Armand. That hope alone keeps me alive. How changed I am. The doctor said that I am very ill. But one may still be very ill and have a few more months to live. If only Armand would come and save me. It is the first day of the new year; a day to hope and look forward in. *(Laughter is heard outside the window.)* I hear people laughing far away.

NANINE. *(entering)* Madame...

MARGUERITE. Yes, Nanine?

NANINE. You feel better today, don't you?

MARGUERITE. Why?

NANINE. If I tell you something, will you promise to keep quite calm and quiet?

MARGUERITE. What is it?

NANINE. I want to prepare you. I'm afraid a sudden joy might kill you.

MARGUERITE. Did you say a joy, Nanine?

NANINE. Yes.

MARGUERITE. Armand! You've seen Armand? He's coming to see me?

*(**NANINE** nods and gives **MARGUERITE** a bunch of camellias.)*

He mustn't see me like this. My hair, bring me a brush. Help me up.

NANINE. No, Madame, you must not get up. You're too weak.

MARGUERITE. *(adamant)* Don't just stand there, help me, Nanine.

*(**NANINE** supports **MARGUERITE** as she struggles over to her vanity table and paints her lips and cheeks.)*

Please, Nanine. Ma solitaire. Ne pas le gros, l'énorme. My camellias. There isn't much time. Send him in, hurry!

*(**DUVAL SR.** appears in the doorway.)*

DUVAL. Madame, you have kept your word to the utmost limit of your strength, and I fear recent events have injured your health. I have written to Armand, telling him the whole story. He was far away but he has returned to ask your forgiveness, not only for himself but for me, too. Go to her, Armand!

MARGUERITE. At last, Armand! It's not possible that you've come back, that God has been so good to me.

ARMAND. If we had not seen Nanine. I should have remained outside and never dared to come near you. Have pity, Marguerite! Don't curse me! If I had not found you again, I should have died because it would have been I who killed you. My father has told me everything. Tell me that you forgive us both. Oh, how good it is to see you again!

MARGUERITE. Forgive you, darling! It was all my fault! But what could I do? I wanted your happiness so much more than my own. Your father won't part us again, will he? You do not see the Marguerite that you used to know, Dear, but I am still young. I will grow beautiful again now that I am happy.

ARMAND. I will never leave you again, Marguerite. We will go to the country at once and never come back to Paris anymore. My father knows what you are now, and will love you as the good angel of his son. My sister is married. The future is ours.

MARGUERITE. We must lose no time, beloved. Life was slipping away from me, but you came and it stayed. You haven't heard, have you? Nichette is to be married, this morning, to Gustave. Let's go to see her married.

ARMAND. And repeat those vows along with them, silently, in our hearts.

MARGUERITE. It would be so good to go to church, to pray to God, and look on a little at the happiness of others. Tell me again that you love me.

ARMAND. I love you, Marguerite. All my life is yours.

MARGUERITE. Bring my outdoor thing, Nanine. I want to go out.

ARMAND. You are a good girl, Nanine. You have taken faithful care of her. Thank you.

MARGUERITE. We used to speak of you every day. No one else dared mention your name. But Nanine would comfort me and tell me that I would see you again. And she was right. You have traveled a long way and seen many strange lands with strange customs. You must tell me about them and perhaps take me there one day. *(She sways.)*

ARMAND. What is it, Marguerite? You are ill!

MARGUERITE. *(with difficulty)* No, it's nothing. Happiness hurts a little at first and my heart has been desolate for so long. *(She throws back her head.)*

ARMAND. Marguerite, speak to me. Marguerite!

MARGUERITE. *(coming to herself)* Don't be afraid, Dear. I always used to have these moments of faintness, don't you remember?

ARMAND. *(taking her hand)* You are trembling!

MARGUERITE. It's nothing. Come, Nanine, give me my shawl and bonnet. We're going to the country! *(NANINE begins to weep.)* Don't just stand there, Nanine. Hurry, we're going to the country! *(tries to walk)* I can't. I can't. I can't.

(MARGUERITE drops. ARMAND catches her and carries her to the chaise.)

ARMAND. *(in terror)* Oh God! Oh, my God! Run for the doctor, Nanine! At once!

MARGUERITE. Yes, yes! Tell him that Armand has come back! That I want to live! That I must live...

(exit NANINE)

But if your coming hasn't saved me, nothing will. I have lived for love. Now I'm dying of it. *(She coughs up blood...sight gag.)*

ARMAND. Hush, Marguerite. You will live. You must.

MARGUERITE. Sit down here beside me, as close as you can. Just for a moment. I was angry at death. But now I see that it had to come. I'm not angry anymore because it has waited long enough for me to see you again. If I had not been going to die, your father would never have written to you to come back.

ARMAND. Marguerite, don't talk like that! I can't bear it! Tell me that you are not going to die! That you don't believe it, that you will not die!

MARGUERITE. Even if I did not wish it, Dear, it would have to be because it is God's will. If I had really been the girl you should have loved, I might have grieved more at leaving a world where you are and a future so full of promise. Then we might have lived happily ever after. But perhaps it's better that I die. Then there'll be no stain on our love. Believe me, God sees more clearly than we do.

ARMAND. Don't! Marguerite, don't.

MARGUERITE. Must I be the one to give you courage? Come, do as I tell you. On my vanity table you will find a miniature of me, painted in the days when I was still pretty. Keep it, it will help your memory later. If ever you should love and marry some young and beautiful girl, as I hope you may one day, and if she should find the portrait and ask who it is, tell her it is a friend who, if God in her starry heaven permits, will never cease to pray for you and her. And if she should be jealous of the past, because we women sometimes are, and ask you to give up the picture, do so, Dearest. I forgive you now, already. A woman suffers too deeply when she feels she is not loved....Are you listening, Armand, my darling, do you hear me?

(Enter **NICHETTE**, *timidly at first and then more boldly as she sees* **MARGUERITE** *smiling and* **ARMAND** *at her feet.)*

NICHETTE. Marguerite, you wrote to me that you were dying, but I find you up and smiling.

ARMAND. *(aside)* Ah, Nichette, I am so miserable!

MARGUERITE. I am dying, but I am happy too, and it is only my happiness that you can see....And so you are married!...Look at that....What a strange life this first one is. What will the second be?...You will be even happier than you were before. Speak of me sometimes, won't you? Armand, give me your hand. Believe me, it's not hard to die. That's strange.

(enter **GASTON***)*

Here is Gaston come back for me! I am so glad to see you again, dear Gaston. Happiness is ungrateful. I had forgotten you....Thank you for filling my purse with money....He has been so good to me, so kind...Ah!...It's strange.

ARMAND. What?

MARGUERITE. I'm not suffering anymore. I feel better, so much better than I have ever felt before...I am going to live. *(She rises from the bed in ecstasy. She glides down center, then collapses into* **ARMAND***'s arms as if asleep.)*

GASTON. She is asleep.

ARMAND. *(with anxiety at first, then with terror)* Marguerite! Marguerite! Marguerite! Don't leave me! Please don't leave me!

GASTON. She loved you dearly, poor girl.

NICHETTE. *(on her knees beside* **MARGUERITE***)* Much will be forgiven you, for you loved much. Toodle-oo, Marguerite.

(Tableau vivant. All lights dim out leaving the little statue of the Madonna on **MARGUERITE***'s vanity in the flickering light of a votive candle.)*

(curtain)

Also by
Charles Ludlam...

The Artificial Jungle
Big Hotel
Bluebeard
Caprice
A Christmas Carol
Conquest of the Universe or When Queens Collide
Corn
Der Ring Gott Farblonjet
The Enchanted Pig
Eunuchs of the Forbidden City
Exquisite Torture
Galas
The Grand Tarot
Hot Ice
How to Write a Play
Isle of the Hermaphrodites or the Murdered Minion
Jack and the Beanstalk
Le Bourgeois Avent-Garde
Love's Tangled Web
Medea
The Mystery of Irma Vep - A Penny Dreadful
Reverse Psychology
Salammbo
Secret Lives of the Sexists
Stage Blood
Turds in Hell
Utopia Incorporated
The Ventriloquist's Wife

Please visit our website **samuelfrench.com** for complete descriptions and licensing information.

OTHER TITLES AVAILABLE FROM SAMUEL FRENCH

THE MYSTERY OF IRMA VEP - A PENNY DREADFUL

Charles Ludlam

Comedy / 2m playing various roles / Simple Set

This definitive spoof of Gothic melodramas, recently revived Off Broadway to raves, is a quick change marathon in which two actors play all the roles. A sympathetic werewolf, a vampire and an Egyptian princess brought to life when her tomb is opened make this a comedy that has everything.

"Far and away the funniest two hours on a New York stage…What more meaningful gift could Ludlam bequeath [audiences] than to leave them eternally laughing."
– *The New York Times*

"A really good laugh…The story has to be seen to be believed."
– *The New York Post*

"Lunatic fun that keeps you in stitches."
– *The New York Daily News*

"A true vaudeville tour de farce…It's wonderful."
– *Time*

"A hearty mixture of thrills, laughter and extravagant showmanship."
– *The Village Voice*

SAMUELFRENCH.COM

OTHER TITLES AVAILABLE FROM SAMUEL FRENCH

CAPRICE

Charles Ludlam

Comedy / 6m, 5f, extras, double casting and cross-gender casting possible / Various Interiors

The comical and tragical history of Claude Caprice, tastemaker and couturier, from the master of the Ridiculous!

Caprice introduces Babushka, the world's first live fashion model, the bra-called "freedom," the "gownless evening strap," and the ultimate fashion statement – sackcloth and ashes – in his keen competition with arch-rival Twyfibrd Adamant, who uses Tata, a fashion spy, to undermine Caprice and his lover Adrian. Baroness Zuni Feinschmecker is a slave of fashion, and her husband Harry discovers the world of fashion – and a new sexual identity – in the House of Caprice.

Caprice is a comic delight, containing a uniquely unapologetic presentation of overtly homosexual characters. The Ballet du Macquillage – a dance for lipstick, powder, rouge, and mascara – is not to be missed.

SAMUELFRENCH.COM

OTHER TITLES AVAILABLE FROM SAMUEL FRENCH

CONQUEST OF THE UNIVERSE
OR
WHEN QUEENS COLLIDE

Charles Ludlam

Comedy / 7m, 8f, extras, double casting and cross-gender casting possible) / Various Settings

Another collage epic by the master of The Ridiculous Theatre, a futuristic tale of war across the universe!

Tamberlaine, President of Earth, proceeds from planet to planet, capturing and enslaving Bajazeth and Zabina – King and Queen of Mars – Venus, and Natolia, Queen of Saturn, among others. Cosroe, a Martian prince and twin brother of Zabina, leads the rebel forces against Tamberlaine in Ludlam's mind-bendingexperimental classic, his theater of "sexual, imperialistic war." Literary, film, and dramatic treasures are ransacked and pillaged for the hilarious dialogue and multiple plots in this unbridled original, humorous tale of unbridled space queens!

SAMUELFRENCH.COM

www.ingramcontent.com/pod-product-compliance
Lightning Source LLC
Chambersburg PA
CBHW070650300426
44111CB00013B/2348